P9-CRZ-675

Waging Peace

Waging Peace

Selections from the Bahá'í Writings
on Universal Peace

A Compilation of the Words of
Bahá'u'lláh, 'Abdu'l-Bahá, and Shoghi Effendi

KALIMÁT PRESS
LOS ANGELES

Extracts from the following works reprinted by permission: By Bahá'u'lláh: *Gleanings from the Writings of Bahá'u'lláh*, Copyright 1939, 1952, © 1976, by the National Spiritual Assembly of the Bahá'ís of the United States. By 'Abdu'l-Bahá: *The Secret of Divine Civilization*, Copyright 1957, © 1970, by the National Spiritual Assembly of the Bahá'ís of the United States; *The Promulgation of Universal Peace*, Copyright © 1982 by the National Spiritual Assembly of the Bahá'ís of the United States. By Shoghi Effendi: *The World Order of Bahá'u'lláh*, Copyright 1938, 1955, © 1974, by the National Spiritual Assembly of the Bahá'ís of the United States. Extracts from *Abdul Baha In London* reprinted by permission of the Bahá'í Publishing Trust of the United Kingdom. Extracts reprinted by permission from *Paris Talks: Addresses Delivered by 'Abdu'l-Bahá in Paris 1911-1912*, © Bahá'í Publishing Trust. Extracts reprinted by permission from *Selections from the Writings of 'Abdu'l-Bahá*, © 1978 by the Universal House of Justice.

Library of Congress Cataloging in Publication Data

Bahá' Alláh, 1817–1892.
Waging peace.

1. Peace—Religious aspects—Baha'i Faith—Addresses, essays, lectures. I. 'Abdu'l-Bahá, 1844–1921. II. Shoghi, Effendi. III. Title.
BP360.B94 1985   297'.8917873   84–29715
ISBN 0-933770-34-0

CONTENTS

FOREWORD

The day was hot, unrelieved by a morning breeze or expected coolness from standing in the shadow of the monument's arch. Thirty-eight years after that fateful August morning's searing atom bomb explosion, I stood now in the heat, the natural warmth of the summer sun, in Hiroshima. The peace monument's epitaph carved words meaning: *"Let all the souls here rest in peace, for we shall not repeat the evil."* A stone inscription only. No matter how heartfelt the sentiment, today we seem no closer to the human social and political structures required to preserve world peace. Monuments only preserve hopes and aspirations, a reminder of our past and a guide to our future—but for our present more is needed. Resting in peace is for the dead. The living must wage peace.

Why have we not accomplished more in resolving regional and global conflicts through peaceful negotiation instead of war, force and threats? Many worthy organizations have come into existence dedicated to assisting in the peace process. Their efforts are to be praised and supported by all workers for peace. But the achievement of measurable steps toward world peace still eludes us. Accomplishments toward conflict resolution in one area of the globe are countered by setbacks elsewhere.

How can we go on living happily and forgetfully in a world so precariously organized that we may suffer extinction when available nuclear weaponry is used on purpose or by accident? Questions like these point out what might be called the "birds on the battlefield" phenomenon which has impeded recognition and acceptance of the enormity of what we must now change to attain world peace. Over millenia battles have been fought, the dead strewn on the fields (or cities)—but the birds return unaware to sing to a new day. The carnage is covered, victory goes to the strong, and new generations of children expect to grow up to take their place. This might have been possible in the past, but not today. There is no guarantee of future generations after a war today.

Bahá'ís and others aware of the new age in which we live recognize that world peace must be an outcome of world unity. World unity, a federation of sovereign nations who cede their "right" to make war, must be accomplished before world peace is attainable. And it is to world unity that the Bahá'í spiritual teachings, with their social and political (i.e., administrative) structure, are dedicated.

SHEILA BANANI
SANTA MONICA, CALIFORNIA
AUGUST 1984

From the Writings of
Bahá'u'lláh

The Great Being saith: O well-beloved ones! The tabernacle of unity hath been raised; regard ye not one another as strangers. Ye are the fruits of one tree, and the leaves of one branch. We cherish the hope that the light of justice may shine upon the world and sanctify it from tyranny. If the rulers and kings of the earth, the symbols of the power of God, exalted be His glory, arise and resolve to dedicate themselves to whatever will promote the highest interests of the whole of humanity, the reign of justice will assuredly be established amongst the children of men, and the effulgence of its light will envelop the whole earth.[1]

The Great Being, wishing to reveal the prerequisites of the peace and tranquility of the world and the advancement of its peoples, hath written: The time must come when the imperative necessity for the holding of a vast, an all-embracing assemblage of men will be universally realized. The rulers and kings of the earth must needs attend it, and, participating in its deliberations, must consider such ways and means as will lay the foundations of the world's Great Peace amongst men. Such a peace demandeth that the Great Powers should resolve, for the sake of the tranquility of the peoples of the earth, to be fully reconciled among themselves. Should any king take up arms against another, all should unitedly arise and prevent him. If this be done, the nations of the world will no longer require any armaments, except for the purpose of preserving the security of their realms and of maintaining internal order within their territories. This will ensure the peace and composure of every people, government and nation. We fain would hope that the kings and rulers of the earth, the mirrors of the gracious and almighty name of God, may attain unto this station, and shield mankind from the onslaught of tyranny.[2]

O ye rulers of the earth! Wherefore have ye clouded the radiance of the Sun, and caused it to cease from shining? Hearken unto the counsel given you by the Pen of the Most High, that haply both ye and the poor may attain unto tranquillity and peace. We beseech God to assist the kings of the earth to establish peace on earth. He, verily, doth what He willeth.

O kings of the earth! We see you increasing every year your expenditures, and laying the burden thereof on your subjects. This, verily, is wholly and grossly unjust. Fear the sighs and tears of this Wronged One, and lay not excessive burdens on your peoples. Do not rob them to rear palaces for yourselves; nay rather choose for them that which ye choose for yourselves. Thus We unfold to your eyes that which profiteth you, if ye but perceive. Your people are your treasures. Beware lest your rule violate the commandments of God, and ye deliver your wards to the hands of the robber. By them ye rule, by their means ye subsist, by their aid ye conquer. Yet, how disdainfully ye look upon them! How strange, how very strange!

Now that ye have refused the Most Great Peace, hold ye fast unto this, the Lesser Peace, that haply ye may in some degree better your own condition and that of your dependents.

O rulers of the earth! Be reconciled among

yourselves, that ye may need no more armaments save in a measure to safeguard your territories and dominions. Beware lest ye disregard
the counsel of the All-Knowing, the Faithful.

Be united, O kings of the earth, for thereby
will the tempest of discord be stilled amongst
you, and your peoples find rest, if ye be of them
that comprehend. Should any one among you
take up arms against another, rise ye all against
him, for this is naught but manifest justice.[3]

That one indeed is a man
who, today, dedicateth himself to the service of
the entire human race. The Great Being saith:
Blessed and happy is he that ariseth to promote
the best interests of the peoples and kindreds of
the earth. In another passage He hath proclaimed: It is not for him to pride himself who
loveth his own country, but rather for him who
loveth the whole world. The earth is but one
country, and mankind its citizens.[4]

The All-Knowing Physician hath His finger on the pulse of mankind. He perceiveth the disease, and prescribeth, in His unerring wisdom, the remedy. Every age hath its own problem, and every soul its particular aspiration. The remedy the world needeth in its present-day afflictions can never be the same as that which a subsequent age may require. Be anxiously concerned with the needs of the age ye live in, and center your deliberations on its exigencies and requirements.

We can well perceive how the whole human race is encompassed with great, with incalculable afflictions. We see it languishing on its bed of sickness, sore-tried and disillusioned. They that are intoxicated by self-conceit have interposed themselves between it and the Divine and infallible Physician. Witness how they have entangled all men, themselves included, in the mesh of their devices. They can neither discover the cause of the disease, nor have they any knowledge of the remedy. They have conceived the straight to be crooked, and have imagined their friend an enemy.

Incline your ears to the sweet melody of this Prisoner. Arise, and lift up your voices, that haply they that are fast asleep may be awakened. Say: O ye who are as dead! The Hand of Divine bounty proffereth unto you the Water of Life. Hasten and drink your fill. Whoso hath been re-born in this Day, shall never die; whoso remaineth dead, shall never live.[5]

From the Words of
'Abdu'l-Bahá

On War

This recent war [World War I] has proved to the world and the people that war is destruction while universal peace is construction; war is death while peace is life; war is rapacity and bloodthirstiness while peace is beneficence and humaneness; war is an appurtenance of the world of nature while peace is of the foundation of the religion of God; war is darkness upon darkness while peace is heavenly light; war is the destroyer of the edifice of mankind while peace is the everlasting life of the world of humanity; war is like a devouring wolf while peace is like the angels of heaven; war is the struggle for existence while peace is mutual aid and co-operation among the peoples of the world and the cause of the good-pleasure of the True One in the heavenly realm.

There is not one soul whose conscience does not testify that in this day there is no more important matter in the world than that of universal peace.[6]

Gracious God! . . . how heedless is man! Still do we see his world at war from pole to pole. There is war among the religions; war among the nations; war among the peoples; war among the rulers. What a welcome change would it be, if only these black clouds would lift from off the skies of the world, so that the light of reality could be shed abroad! If only the darksome dust of this continual fighting and killing could settle forever, and the sweet winds of God's loving-kindness could blow from out the well-spring of peace. Then would this world become another world, and the earth would shine with the light of her Lord.

If there is any hope, it is solely in the bounties of God: that His strengthening grace will come, and the struggling and contending will cease, and the acid bite of blood-dripping steel will be turned into the honey-dew of friendship and probity and trust. How sweet would that day be in the mouth, how fragrant as musk the scent thereof.[7]

*H*is Holiness Bahá'u'lláh nearly fifty years ago warned the nations against the occurrence of this "Most Great Danger." Although the evils of war were evident and manifest to the sages and scholars, they are now made clear and plain to all the people. No sane person can at this time deny the fact that war is the most dreadful calamity in the world of humanity, that war destroys the divine foundation, that war is the cause of eternal death, that war is conducive to the destruction of populous, progressive cities, that war is the world-consuming fire, and that war is the most ruinous catastrophe and the most deplorable adversity.

The cries and lamentations are raised from every part to the Supreme Apex; the moanings and shriekings have thrown a mighty reverberation through the columns of the world; the civilized countries are being overthrown; eyes are shedding tears, hearing the weeping of the fatherless children; the hearts are burning and being consumed by uncontrollable sobbings and piercing wailings of helpless, wandering women; the spirits of hopeless mothers are torn by rayless grief and endless sorrows and the nerve-racking sighs and the just complaints of fathers ascend to the Throne of the Almighty.

Ah me! The world of creation is totally deprived of its normal rest; the clash of arms and the sound of murderous guns and cannon are being heard like the roaring of thunder across the heavenly tract, and the explosive materials have changed the battlefields into yawning graveyards, burying for eternity the corpses of thousands upon thousands of youths—the flower of many countries who would have been evolving factors in the civilization of the future.

The results of this crime committed against humanity are worse than whatever I may say and can never be adequately described by pen or by tongue.

O ye governments of the world! Be ye pitiful toward mankind! O ye nations of the earth, behold ye the battlefields of slaughter and carnage; O ye sages of humanity, investigate sympathetically the conditions of the oppressed; O ye philosophers of the West, study profoundly the causes that led to this gigantic, unparalled struggle; O ye wise leaders of the globe, reflect deeply so that ye may find an antidote for the suppression of this chronic, devastating disease; O ye individuals of humanity, find ye means for the stoppage of this wholesale murder and bloodshed. Now is the appointed time! Now is the opportune time! Arise ye, shew ye an effort, put ye forward an extraordinary power, and unfurl ye the Flag of Universal Peace and dam the irresistible fury of this raging torrent which is wreaking havoc and ruin everywhere![8]

$\mathcal{T}$oday in the world of humanity the most important matter is the question of Universal Peace. The realization of this principle is the crying need of the time. People have become restive and discontented. The political world of every civilized nation has become a vast arena for the exhibition of militarism and the display of martial spirit. The minds of the statesmen and Cabinet Ministers of every government are chiefly occupied with the question of war, and the council chambers are resounding with the call to war. Self-interest is at the bottom of every war. Greed, commerce, exploitation, the pushing further of the boundaries of the kingdom, colonization, the preservation of the treaty rights, the safeguarding of the lives and interests of the citizens, are a few of the pretexts of going into war. And it has been proven by experience that the results of war are ruinous, both to the conquerors and the conquered. Countries are laid waste, public property trampled under foot, commerce is paralyzed, fields crimsoned with innocent blood, and the progress of the world retarded. How can a person rectify a wrong by committing a greater wrong—shedding the blood of his brothers? The major part of the revenue of every country is expended over military preparations, infernal engines, the filling of arsenals with powder and shot, the construction of rapid-firing guns, the building of fortifications and soldiers' barracks and the annual maintenance of the army and navy. From the peasants upward every class of society is heavily taxed to feed this insatiable monster of war. The poor people have wrested from them all that they make with the sweat of their brows and the labor of their hands.

In reality war is continuous. The moral effect of the expenditures of these colossal sums of money for military purposes is just as deteriorating as the actual war and its train of dreadful carnage and horrors. The ideal and moral forces of the contending parties become barbaric and bestial, the spiritual powers are stunted and the laws of divine civilization are disregarded. Such a financial drain ossifies the veins and muscles of the body-politic, and congeals the delicate sensibilities of the spirit.

There is not the least doubt that the nation or the government which puts forward an extraordinary effort in the promotion of Universal Peace, will be encircled with Divine Confirmations, and will be the object of honor and respect among all the inhabitants of the earth.[9]

. . . *I* wonder at the human savagery that still exists in the world! How is it possible for men to fight from morning until evening, killing each other, shedding the blood of their fellow-men: And for what object? To gain possession of a part of the earth! Even the animals, when they fight, have an immediate and more reasonable cause for their attacks! How terrible it is that men, who are of the higher kingdom, can descend to slaying and bringing misery to their fellow-beings, for the possession of a tract of land!

The highest of created beings fighting to obtain the lowest form of matter, earth! Land belongs not to one people, but to all people. This earth is not man's home, but his tomb. It is for their tombs these men are fighting. There is nothing so horrible in this world as the tomb, the abode of the decaying bodies of men.

However great the conqueror, however many countries he may reduce to slavery, he is unable to retain any part of these devastated lands but one tiny portion—his tomb! If more land is required for the improvement of the condition of the people, for the spread of civilization (for the substitution of just laws for brutal customs)—surely it would be possible to acquire peaceably the necessary extension of territory.

But war is made for the satisfaction of men's ambition; for the sake of worldly gain to the few, terrible misery is brought to numberless homes, breaking the hearts of hundreds of men and women!

How many widows mourn their husbands, how many stories of savage cruelty do we hear! How many little orphaned children are crying for their dead fathers, how many women are weeping for their slain sons!

There is nothing so heart-breaking and terrible as an outburst of human savagery![10]

'Abdu'l-Bahá: "Everything that prevents war is good."

Hudson Maxim: "Christ said He came to make war. Caesar was great in history because he was great in battle and military skill."

'Abdu'l-Bahá: "We have the history of the world for nearly six thousand years. Before that there is no record. During these six thousand years there has been constant war, strife, bloodshed. We can see at a glance the results, achievements and outcomes of war. The history of warfare and strife is known, the effect apparent. Have we not a sufficient standard of experience in this direction? Let us now try peace for awhile. If good results follow, let us adhere to it. If not let us throw it away and fight again. Nothing will be lost by the experiment."

Hudson Maxim: "Evolution has now reached a period in the life of nations where commerce takes the place of warfare. Business is war, cruel, merciless."

'Abdu'l-Bahá: "True! War is not limited to one cause. There are many kinds of war and conflict going on, political war, commercial war, patriotic and racial war; this is the very civilization of war."

Hudson Maxim: "Do you consider the next great national war necessary?"

'Abdu'l-Bahá: "I hope your efforts may be able to prevent it. Why not try peace for awhile? If we find war is better, it will not be difficult to fight again; but if we find that peace is the glorification of humanity, the impulse of true civilization, the stimulus to inventive genius and the means of attainment to the good-pleasure of God, we must agree to adhere to it and establish it permanently."

Hudson Maxim: ". . . You are right in advocating peace. I am an advocate of peace from another standpoint. I would make war so expensive that the nations could not afford to fight and therefore would agree to maintain peace."

'Abdu'l-Bahá: "The product of human invention, genius and the outcome of human disposition to kill and fight have well-nigh reached their limit. It seems as if the art of war could not be carried further. In ancient times when nation fought against nation, probably one thousand would be killed in battle, the expense would not be great, the outcome of victory decisive and final; but in modern times the science of war has reached such a stage of perfection that in twenty-four hours one-hundred-thousand could be sacrificed, great navies sent to the bottom of the sea, great cities destroyed in a few hours. The possibilities are incalculable, inconceivable, the after effects even more dreadful than the initial shock. In Egypt, the fellaheen who till the Nile banks, gather four or five harvests from the soil. Suppose they are called away from their peaceful pursuits, take up arms, expend their possessions for powder and go to war. The first consequences are grievous enough, but the after-results are even more deplorable. The country suffers beyond all power of estimation; agriculture is crippled, abandoned, sustenance fails, poverty and suffering continue long afterward. Furthermore, how many wars there have been in the Orient during past centuries; war and peace in constant succession; but your country America remained unaffected by them or their consequences. The news of war might reach Europe and America long after it had happened. But all this is changed in the present century. As soon as war is declared in any part of the world, all human attention is directed toward it; commerce and the machinery of nations are paralyzed; the whole world thrown into a condition of grave uncertainty. Therefore it is evident that the time has come to end war and establish peace. This is an exigency and requirement of the present century."[11]

$\mathcal{T}$oday the people are thrown into the utmost consternation! How many fathers were lamenting and groaning last night, and how many mothers have been crying and weeping in this town and 'Akká! They are thrown into such a panic, they are so alarmed that no description can give an adequate picture! Why this tyranny? Who has obliged them to perpetuate these acts of savagery! The kings and the rulers, the politicians and the statesmen live in the utmost ease in their palaces and send these innocent men and peasants who have never seen each other, into the battlefield to tear each other to pieces with shells and cannon balls. The armies are the pawns to be played with on the chess-board of their fiendish ambitions! How cruel is this! How pitiless is this! How brutal is this! How ferocious is this! These so-called leaders of humanity are not willing to let even one hair fall from their heads. They are cowards and are sulking in darkness. Why do they send these thousands and thousands of men to the field of carnage, to be mowed down by each other like the grass! . . .

More astonishing than all these matters is this: These warring nations believe that the object of the religion of God is war and strife! This is the most preposterous idea that any man could let enter into his mind! . . . How negligent are the people! How thoughtless and inadvertent they are! It is as though there is not a single iota of love in the hearts of men, as though they have never heard the name of love, as though their hearts are the sepulchers of hatred and envy! Man is the *most ferocious animal,* yet does he accuse the wild beasts of the jungle of this quality! The ferocious beasts kill other beasts, but not one belonging to their own species. They kill for their own food and sustenance. For example, man says the wolf is ferocious!

O, poor wolf! O, wronged wolf! The wolf tears to pieces one sheep in order to keep its body alive. If it does not kill the sheep, it will die of hunger, because being a carnivorous animal, it cannot eat grass. But man, who considers himself lord of creation, will become the cause of the total annihilation of a million of his fellow-beings. The poor wolf is a very incompetent tyro in comparison with this kind of man! Then he will boast "I am a conqueror, I am a hero, I am a victor, I am a superior General, I am a Field-Marshal, I am an Admiral!"

Man! It is better for thee to hide thy head

under the earth! Thou hast crimsoned the ground with the blood of thy brothers! Thy hand is stained with their blood! Thou hast slaughtered and butchered God's own children! Thou hast destroyed the living temples of the Spirit! Thou hast trampled under thy feet the rights of men! Thou hast snuffed out the burning lamps of life and truth! It is strange, passing strange, that notwithstanding all these violations of Divine Law, thou art yet wantonly boasting and exalting thyself above all mankind.[12]

The Need for Unity

. . . All names which seek to differentiate and distinguish mankind as Italian, German, French, Russian and so on are without significance and sanction. We are all human, all servants of God and all come from Mr. Adam's family. Why, then, all these fallacious national and racial distinctions? These boundary lines and artificial barriers have been created by despots and conquerors who sought to attain dominion over mankind, thereby engendering patriotic feeling and rousing selfish devotion to merely local standards of government. As a rule they themselves enjoyed luxuries in palaces, surrounded by conditions of ease and affluence, while armies of soldiers, civilians and tillers of the soil fought and died at their command upon the field of battle, shedding their innocent blood for a delusion such as "we are Germans," "our enemies are French," etc., when, in reality, all are humankind, all belong to the one family and posterity of Adam, the original father. This prejudice or limited patriotism is prevalent throughout the world, while man is blind to patriotism in the larger sense which includes all races and native lands. From every real standpoint there must and should be peace among all nations.

God created one earth and one mankind to people it. Man has no other habitation, but man himself has come forth and proclaimed imaginary boundary lines and territorial restrictions, naming them Germany, France, Russia, etc. And torrents of precious blood are spilled in defense of these imaginary divisions of our one human habitation, under the delusion of a fancied and limited patriotism.

After all, a claim and title to territory or

native land is but a claim and attachment to the dust of earth. We live upon this earth for a few days and then rest beneath it forever. So it is our graveyard eternally. Shall man fight for the tomb which devours him, for his eternal sepulcher? What ignorance could be greater than this? To fight over his grave, to kill another for his grave! What heedlessness! What a delusion![13]

Man should endeavor always to realize the Oneness of Humanity. We are all the children of God; all created by God; all provided for by God and all under the protection of God. God is kind to all His children. Why should they wage war between themselves? God is the Real Shepherd—all are His sheep. There is no difference whatever among the members of the flock. He educates all of us, is compassionate to all of us; protects all of us. Ponder and you will understand that with the bounties of God there is no restraint. His grace encompasses all mankind. All live under His bounty.

What benefit do we ever draw from separating ourselves one from another? Why should we wrangle and battle to kill each other? God is kind. Why are we unkind?

The first separating principle is religion. Every sect and community has gathered around itself certain imitations of Reality in ceremonies and forms, and as these imitations differ, contentions follow. Each division is encompassed with thick clouds through which the Sun of Reality cannot penetrate. If these divisions should forget the differences in imitations and seek for the underlying Reality, all would be united and agreed and fellowship would be established between the organizations of mankind.

As His Holiness Mohammed states, "God is Love upon Love, with Love." Therefore it is evident that the foundation of Religion is Love and the fundamental purpose of religion is Unity. The Religion of God is honor to humanity; why make it the cause of degradation? Why make it the cause of darkness and gloom? Assuredly it is a thousand pities that the cause of such a glorious reality should become the cause of degradation and hatred.

It was at a time of great darkness that His

Holiness Bahá'u'lláh appeared in Persia, summoning all to love and friendship. Now, in Persia, Jews, Christians, Zoroastrians and other contending religionists who heard the words of Bahá'u'lláh are living in the utmost state of love and reciprocity.

This Cause is great and it was at great cost that Bahá'u'lláh strove to spread these principles in the world. During His life He was imprisoned, His property was pillaged. He was separated from His friends and 20,000 of His followers were martyred. They sacrificed their lives in the glorious cause of doing away with imitations and limitations, to this end that Unity might be established among the children of men.[14]

$\mathcal{F}$ifty years ago Bahá'u'lláh declared the necessity of peace among the nations and the reality of reconciliation between the religions of the world. He announced that the fundamental basis of all religion is one, that the essence of religion is human fellowship and that the differences in belief which exist are due to dogmatic interpretation and blind imitations which are at variance with the foundations established by the Prophets of God. He proclaimed that if the reality underlying religious teaching be investigated all religions would be unified, and the purpose of God, which is love and the blending of human hearts, would be accomplished. According to His teachings if religious belief proves to be the cause of discord and dissension, its absence would be preferable; for religion was intended to be the divine remedy and panacea for the ailments of humanity, the healing balm for the wounds of mankind. If its misapprehension and defilement have brought about warfare and bloodshed instead of remedy and cure, the world would be better under irreligious conditions.[15]

$\mathcal{R}$eligion should unite all hearts and cause wars and disputes to vanish from the face of the earth, give birth to spirituality, and bring life and light to each heart. If religion becomes a cause of dislike, hatred and division, it were better to be without it, and to withdraw from such a religion would be a truly religious act. For it is clear that the purpose of a remedy is to cure; but if the remedy should only aggravate the complaint it had better be left alone. Any religion which is not a cause of love and unity is no religion. All the holy prophets were as doctors to the soul; they gave prescriptions for the healing of mankind; thus any remedy that causes disease does not come from the great and supreme Physician.[16]

Those Who Work for Peace

While traveling in Europe and America I met altruistic and sanctified souls who were my confidants and associates concerning the question of Universal Peace and who agreed with me and joined their voices with mine regarding the principle of the Oneness of the World of Humanity; but alas, they were very few! The leaders of public opinion and the great statesmen believed that the massing of huge armies and the annual increase of military forces insured peace and friendship among nations. At that time I explained that this theory was based on a false conception; for it is an inevitable certainty that these serried ranks and disciplined armies will be rushed one day into the heat of the battlefield and these inflammable materials will unquestionably be exploded and the explosion will be through one tiny spark; then a world conflagration will be witnessed, the lurid flames of which shall redden all the horizons. Because the sphere of their thoughts was contracted and their intellectual eyes blind they could not acknowledge the above explanation.[17]

There is the well-known case of the ruler who is fostering peace and tranquillity and at the same time devoting more energy than the warmongers to the accumulation of weapons and the building up of a larger army, on the grounds that peace and harmony can only be brought about by force. Peace is the pretext, and night and day they are all straining every nerve to pile up more weapons of war, and to pay for this their wretched people must sacrifice most of whatever they are able to earn by their sweat and toil. How many thousands have given up their work in useful industries and are laboring day and night to produce new and deadlier weapons which would spill out the blood of the race more copiously than before.[18]

$\mathcal{I}$n these days the world of humanity is afflicted with a chronic disease. It is one of bloodshed, the destruction of the divine edifice, the demolition of cities and villages, the slaughter of the noble youths of the world of humanity, children becoming orphans and women homeless and shelterless. What calamity is greater than this? What crime is more heinous than this? What disease is more dangerous than this? What folly is more direful than this?

Consider that in former days there were only religious wars, but now there are racial and political wars fought at staggering expense and sacrifice. A thousand times alas for this ignorance, this bloodthirstiness and ferocity! I became pleased with and grateful to the societies which are organized in the West for the promotion of universal peace, and with whose presidents, officers and members I frequently conversed. I hope that the sphere of the activities of these societies may become from day to day enlarged; so that the lights of the higher ideals may illumine all regions, the oneness of the world of humanity be proclaimed in the East and in the West, and the world of humanity may attain to composure and well-being. These revered souls who are the servants of the world of humanity and the promoters of the cause of universal peace shall ere long shine like brilliant stars from the horizon of mankind, flooding the regions with their glorious lights.[19]

*T*ruly I say many societies are organized in America for the promotion of the thought of peace and universal brotherhood. That country has preceded all the rest in this respect. But all these peace societies organized in the countries of the West, whose aim is the oneness of the realm of humanity, consist of explanations and theories on this subject; but the Bahá'ís have engraved this matter on the page of this world with their own blood. Through the power of the Word of God they have unfurled the banner of the oneness of the kingdom of humanity upon the apex of the world with deeds and actions; and through the bounty of Bahá'u'lláh they have spread the proclamation of the brotherhood of man and the universal equality among the people of the East and the West. Herein consists the difference.

Consider thou that the Hague Conference was instituted and established by the kings and rulers of the world, but when it came to the station of action, the Czar of Russia, who was the founder of the Conference, declared war with Japan. Nearly one million of souls were torn to pieces on the battlefield and kneaded the earth with their blood. Notwithstanding this, the Bahá'ís must associate and become members of these peace societies, so that they may awaken them to the realization that this great cause of universal peace cannot be established and maintained except through the power of God, which is supernatural.

Human nature in this phenomenal world is fashioned with the poison of war and strife. We need a powerful force beyond and above this world of nature, so that this condition may be effaced from the surface of the world.[20]

. . . The well-wishers of the world of humanity and the advocates of universal peace must make an extraordinary forward movement, organize important international congresses, and invite as delegates most progressive and influential souls from all parts of the world; so that through their wise counsels and deliberations this ideal of Universal Peace may leap out of the world of words into the arena of actuality and practical demonstration. It is true that this question is of paramount importance, and will not be realized easily. However, we must take hold of every means until the desired result is obtained.

Fifty years ago whosoever talked about Universal Peace was not only ridiculed but called a visionary and utopian. Now—praise be to God!—that at this time it has assumed such importance that everyone acknowledges that this question of Universal Peace is the light and spirit of this age. But they state that the pathway to this much desired goal is obstructed by a number of not clearly defined stumbling blocks, which, however, can be removed by intelligently and persistently educating public opinion.[21]

*A*ll of us know that international peace is good, that it is conducive to human welfare and the glory of man, but volition and action are necessary before it can be established. Action is essential. Inasmuch as this century is a century of light, capacity for action is assured to mankind. Necessarily the divine principles will be spread among men until the time of action arrives. Surely this has been so, and truly the time and conditions are ripe for action now. All men know that, verily, war is a destroyer of human foundations, and in every country of the world this is admitted and apparent. I find the United States of America an exceedingly progressive nation, the government just, the people in a state of readiness and the principle of equality established to an extraordinary degree. Therefore, it is my hope that, inasmuch as the standard of international peace must be upraised, it may be upraised upon this continent, for this nation is more deserving and has greater capacity for such an initial step than any other.[22]

$\mathcal{T}$oday, upon the earth, one sees the sad spectacle of cruel war! Man slays his brother man for selfish gain, and to enlarge his territories! For this ignoble ambition hate has taken possession of his heart, and more and more blood is shed!

Fresh battles are fought, the armies are increased, more cannon, more guns, more explosives of all kinds are sent out—so does bitterness and hate augment from day to day!

But this assembly, thank God, longs only for peace and unity, and must work with heart and soul to bring about a better condition in the world.

You who are the servants of God fight against

oppression, hate and discord, so that wars may cease and God's laws of peace and love may be established among men.

Work! Work with all your strength, spread the Cause of the Kingdom among men; teach the self-sufficient to turn humbly towards God, the sinful to sin no more, and await with glad expectation the coming of the Kingdom.

Love and obey your Heavenly Father, and rest assured that Divine help is yours. Verily I say unto you that you shall indeed conquer the world![23]

'Abdu'l-Bahá: "You are very welcome; I am most happy to greet you. I have looked forward with much pleasure to this meeting. Welcome! Welcome!"

Mr. W. H. Short, Secretary of the New York Peace Society: "It gives me great happiness indeed to meet 'Abdu'l-Bahá. I too have looked forward to this meeting. The New York Peace Society extends him greetings and welcome to our city and our country."

'Abdu'l-Bahá: "You are indeed a servant to

humanity. A servant to humanity is a servant to God. Your mission is a high, holy and sanctified one; there could be no greater, no holier mission than that of bringing peace to this warring world. Therefore I have waited for you with the greatest longing.

"In this day the majority of mankind are endeavoring to destroy the foundations of the happiness of the world. How many are engaged in the invention of means for the destruction of human kind; how many are employed in the science and practice of war; how many are occupied in various kinds of strife and antagonism; how many stand ready to shed the blood of innocent men, their brothers! So it is that history is blackened with this record of human intention and accomplishment. Every hour war is threatened upon some new pretext; today patriotism is its basis, tomorrow religious prejudice, racial egotism, territorial greed, commercial selfishness—it matters little what the excuse may be—blood is shed and human beings torn to pieces upon battlefields. Political interests clash; a great war follows; sadness, gloom and cruelty envelop the world.

"But you are endeavoring to uplift the standard of peace in the world. You must continue to work until the world is released from these prejudices which are bringing about such inhuman conditions. For the clouds of war will surely vanish from the horizons. There is no doubt that your work is the greatest work and its outcome certain.''

Mr. Short: ''All the members of the New York Peace Society feel the truth and inspiration of what you have said.''

'Abdu'l-Bahá: ''You must rest assured and let there be no traces of doubt in your souls that God is your Assister and Helper. The Heavenly confirmations will descend upon you more and more. God will protect you and give you new strength continually. Your world-motives will conquer the world of men; all obstacles will disappear before your advance; no earthly power can resist the onrushing power of Peace.''[24]

The Bahá'í Peace Program

The peoples of Europe have not advanced to the higher planes of moral civilization, as their opinions and behavior clearly demonstrate. Notice, for example, how the supreme desire of European governments and peoples today is to conquer and crush one another, and how, while harboring the greatest secret repulsion, they spend their time exchanging expressions of neighborly affection, friendship and harmony. . . .

Each day they invent a new bomb or explosive and then the governments must abandon their obsolete arms and begin producing the new, since the old weapons cannot hold their own against the new. For example at this writing, in the year [1875], they have invented a new rifle in Germany and a bronze cannon in Austria, which have greater firepower than the Martini-Henry rifle and the Krupp cannon, are more rapid in their effects and more efficient in annihilating humankind. The staggering cost of it all must be borne by the hapless masses. . . .

At the time of the Franco-Prussian War, in the year 1870 of the Christian era, it was reported that 600,000 men died, broken and beaten, on the field of battle. How many a home was torn out by the roots; how many a city, flourishing the night before, was toppled down by sunrise. How many a child was orphaned and abandoned, how many an old father and mother had to see their sons, the young fruit of their lives, twisting and dying in dust and blood. How many women were widowed, left without a helper or protector.

And then there were the libraries and magnificent buildings of France that went up in flames, and the military hospital, packed with sick and wounded men, that was set on fire and burned to the ground. And there followed the terrible events of the Commune, the savage acts, the ruin and horror when opposing factions fought and killed one another in the streets of Paris. There were the hatreds and hostilities between Catholic religious leaders and the German government. There was the civil strife and uproar, the bloodshed and havoc brought on between the partisans of the Republic and the Carlists in Spain.

Only too many such instances are available to demonstrate the fact that Europe is morally uncivilized.[25]

How is universal peace to be established? By the education of the public with the sentiments of peace. Today the full realization of universal peace is the panacea of every disease.

What are the diseases?

One of the diseases is the impoverishment of the farmers and the middle classes through the unbearable burden of war taxes.

This wave of military craze has reached its height. It shall soon recede. The income of the farmers and others is taken by the force of a military government and expended foolishly over useless instruments of destruction. The prospect of every government becomes gloomier every year, because the war budget of every government is being increased without regard to the feverish signs of social unrest and industrial upheavals. The people are seething with ideas of insurrection and agitation. The burden has become too heavy. The patience of mankind is exhausted. They groan under this load, and they grope in the darkness seeking the light of peace and brotherhood. Their pitiful cries ascend to the throne of the Almighty. Lo! Lo! He has listened to them; He has answered their prayers. The dawn of peace hath appeared. The lights of brotherhood are breaking through the dark clouds of human prejudices. Lovers of peace, rejoice! O ye who are heavy laden, be happy, be happy! Weep no more, for your loads will be taken from you!

This military and naval expenditure is a great disease. Look at the results of the war between Italy and Turkey how dreadful they are! The fathers hear the news of the death of their sons. The sons are grieved through the death of their fathers. How many peaceful villages are laid waste! How the wealth of two nations is exhausted!

The remedy of this disease is through universal peace. This will insure public safety. Today that which is the cause of dispersion is war. If the nations enter into a faithful agreement to leave off all war-like preparations at once, they shall secure for themselves and their posterity eternal welfare. They shall become freed from every difficulty and international confusion. This end must be obtained through the development of the intellects and the inculcation of peaceful ideals in all the institutions of modern civilization.[26]

𝒩early sixty years ago when the horizon of the Orient was in a state of the utmost gloom, warfare existed and there was enmity between the various creeds; darkness brooded over the children of men and foul clouds of ignorance hid the sky—at such a time His Highness Bahá'u'lláh arose from the horizon of Persia like unto a shining sun. He boldly proclaimed peace, writing to the kings of the earth and calling upon them to arise and assist in the hoisting of this banner. In order to bring peace out of the chaos, he established certain precepts or principles:

Investigations of Truth. The first principle Bahá'u'lláh urged was the independent investigation of truth. "Each individual," he said, "is following the faith of his ancestors who themselves are lost in the maze of tradition. Reality is steeped in dogmas and doctrines. If each investigate for himself, he will find that Reality is one; does not admit of multiplicity; is not divisible. All will find the same foundation and all will be at peace."

The Unity of the Race. The second principle of Bahá'u'lláh proclaims the oneness of the human race. He states that humanity constitute the sheep of God. God is the real shepherd. When this shepherd is compassionate and kind, why should the sheep quarrel amongst themselves? Addressing all humanity, Bahá'u'lláh says, ''Ye are the fruits of one tree and the leaves of one branch. All the nations, peoples and tongues are the branches, leaves, blossoms and fruits of this great tree of humanity.'' God created all; protects all; provides for all and is kind to all; why should you be unkind? If God had not loved humanity He would not have created it. Creation presupposes love. God is the real father; all are His children. All the creatures are equal in this one family of God save whosoever is more kind, more compassionate,—he is nearer to God.

International Peace. The third principle of the religion of Bahá'u'lláh is in regard to international peace. There must be peace between the fatherlands; peace between the religions. In this period of evolution the world of humanity is in danger. Every war is against the good pleasure of the Lord of mankind. Man is the edifice of God. War destroys the divine edifice. Peace is the stay of life; war the cause of death. If an active, actual peace is brought about, the human world will attain to the utmost serenity and composure. Wolves will be transformed into lambs; devils into angels and terrors into divine splendors in less than the twinkling of an eye.

Religion Must Conform to Science and Reason. The fourth principle declares that religion must be in conformity to science and reason. If a religion does not agree with the postulates of science nor accord with the regulations of reason it is a bundle of superstitions; a phantasm of the brain. Science and religion are realities, and if that religion to which we adhere be a reality it must needs conform to the fundamental reality of all things.

Prejudice Must Be Forever Banished. The fifth principle of Bahá'u'lláh is this: that religious, racial, political and patriotic prejudice are the destroyers of human society. As long as these prejudices last the world of humanity will not attain to poise and perfection. As long as these threatening clouds are in the sky of humanity, the sun of reality cannot dawn.

Equality of Sexes. The sixth principle of Bahá'u'lláh regards the equality of men and women. The male and female of the human kingdom are equal before God. God is no respecter of gender. Whosoever practices more faith, whosoever practices more humanitarianism is nearer to God; but between the male and female there is no innate difference because

47

they share in common all the faculties. The world of humanity has two wings, one the male; the other the female. When both wings are reinforced with the same impulse the bird will be enabled to wing its flight heavenward to the summit of progress. Woman must be given the same opportunities as man for perfecting herself in the attainments of learning, science and arts. God has created the man and the woman equal, why should she be deprived of exercising the fullest opportunities afforded by life? Why should we ever raise the question of superiority and inferiority? In the animal kingdom the male and female enjoy suffrage [laughter], and in the vegetable kingdom the plants all enjoy equal suffrage [laughter and applause]. In the human kingdom, which claims to be the realm of brotherhood and solidarity, why should we raise this question?

The Social Plan. The seventh teaching suggests a plan whereby all the individual members may enjoy the utmost comfort and welfare. The degrees of society must be preserved. The farmer will continue to till the soil, the artist pursue his art, the banker to finance the nation. An army has need of its general, captain, and private soldiers. The degrees varying with the pursuits are essential. But in this Bahá'í plan there is no class hatred. Each is to be protected and each individual member of the body politic is to live in the greatest comfort and happiness. Work is to be provided for all and there will be no needy ones to be seen in the streets.

The Parliament of Man. The eighth principle declares that there must needs be established the parliament of man or court of last appeals for international questions. The members of this arbitral court of justice will be representatives of all the nations. In each nation the members must be ratified by the government and the king or ruler, and this international parliament will be under the protection of the world of humanity. In it all international difficulties will be settled.

Universal Education. The ninth admonition is in regard to education. All the children must be educated so that there will not remain one single individual without an education. In cases of inability on the part of the parents through sickness, death, etc., the state must educate the child. In addition to this widespread education, each child must be taught a profession or trade so that each individual member of the body politic will be enabled to earn his own living and at the same time serve the community. Work done in the spirit of service is worship. From this universal system of education misunderstandings will be expelled from amongst the children of men.

Universal Language. The tenth principle is the establishment of a universal language so that we will not have to acquire so many languages in the future. In the schools they will study two, the mother tongue and the international auxiliary language. The use of an international auxiliary language will become a great means of dispelling the differences between nations.

There are many other teachings. I have given you but a few. Praise be to God! that day by day we are advancing and every day we see some new blessing descending. Let all of us render thanksgiving to our generous Lord that He may bless our eyes with sight and give unto our hearts understanding. May we become resuscitated with the breath of the Holy Spirit. May we be enabled to leave behind the world of matter in beholding the bounties of God. The divine table is spread, the heavenly illumination is all-encircling; eternal life is provided for all; divine food is prepared for all! Therefore let us practice the divine essence of love and love each other from our very hearts and souls so that the East and West shall embrace each other and realize that all are the sheep of God. God is the good shepherd—then will we gather under the tabernacle of His mercy![27]

Consider carefully that for the last six thousand years there has been constant strife and warfare amongst the people. All the wars which have occurred in past history have been the basis of the destruction of the human race; love, on the other hand, has been the cause of cementing the people together. . . .

In order that the darkness of strife and sedition might be entirely banished from the human world, His Holiness Bahá'u'lláh established and taught certain declarations or principles. The first principle which He proclaimed was the principle of the Oneness of the human family. He said, "Humanity constitute the sheep of God's flock. The real shepherd is God." The real shepherd is compassionate and kind towards all the members of his flock. Humanity was created by God; He provides for all, protects all. He is kind to all. Why should we treat each other harshly? He has made a plea for love, not for difference, or hatred, or animosity.

God created humanity; none of us were created by Satan. All are edifices of God, therefore we must strive that these edifices be protected and not seek to destroy them.

The second principle of Bahá'u'lláh concerns international peace and to this end He wrote all the nations and sent special epistles to the rulers and kings of the earth. Likewise He proclaimed peace amongst the religions. Was not peace the foundations of religion? It is time that these limitations and dogmas be done away with, that the foundation of the religion of God be made the means of union and good fellowship.

Again, He proclaimed interracial peace, for humanity is the progeny of one Adam—all belong to one lineage. "This sphere is one globe," He said, and is not divided, the various continents on the face of the globe are in reality one native land, inhabited by one human family; therefore, there should not exist between the various countries this warfare and strife.

Another principle of Bahá'u'lláh is that religion must ever be the means of love; that is, if so-called religion be the cause of hatred and animosity, it is better to quit such religion. Every affair, every matter which in the world of humanity is the cause of love, that matter is good; but if it is creative of difference amongst the children of men, that matter is evil. If it be a cause of hatred amongst the people, it is absolute evil. Irreligion is better than that so-called religion. The people have made religion the cause of warfare and strife, while the reality of religion is the cause of unity and love.

The fourth teaching of Bahá'u'lláh is relative to the conformity of science and reason with true universal religion. If it is contrary to science and reason, it is superstition. A theory which is not acceptable to the mind of man and which science rejects is devoid of reality. It is a vision of superstition.

The fifth teaching of Bahá'u'lláh is relative to prejudice, which must be abandoned. National prejudice must be forgotten, racial prejudice must be obliterated, and patriotic prejudice must likewise be lifted from amongst the people.

Since the beginning of history all the wars which have occurred have been caused primarily through religious prejudice, or racial prejudice, or patriotic prejudice. As long as these prejudices are not broken, the world of humanity will not attain to perfect peace and tranquillity.

Another teaching of Bahá'u'lláh is relative to the equality of men and women. In the human family of God there is no distinction. God is no respecter of gender. The religion of God is one.

The human family share in common all the faculties; they share in common all the divine bounties. God has not accredited any difference between the male and the female. The same education must be given to women as to men, so that they may acquire science and arts, so that they may advance along the course of civilization, in order that they may become proficient and attain to the level of men.

In the Orient women have been very degraded in the past, men giving no importance to them, thinking that men were created superior, but through the teaching of Bahá'u'lláh, who declared that a great calling is destined for women, they promoted the facilities for the education and training of the girls. In a brief space of time the girls and the women alike have advanced along the pathway of education. Now, in the country of Persia alone, many schools have been organized for the girls, and girls are engaged in the study of the sciences and arts.

The seventh teaching of Bahá'u'lláh concerns itself and is in accord with this system of universal education; it is that all the children should study and acquire a profession, that there should not remain a single individual without a profession whereby he can earn his livelihood.

Bahá'u'lláh further declares that through the equipment of science and art the misunderstandings which have prevailed between religion and science will become reconciled.

The non-conformity of science and religion has been the greatest factor in keeping the religions apart.

If this misunderstanding be taken away from amongst religions, perfect love will be established. For example, for nearly two thousand years there has been strife and contention between Jews and Christians and it is evident that if the cause thereof be understood with intelligence, it would wipe away from among them all discord; there would remain love and concord. . . .

The paramount declaration of Bahá'u'lláh is that peace must be realized between all the nations of the Earth. International tribunals will be established and certain representatives from amongst all the governments of the earth will be sent to that inter-parliamentary gathering. The era of "the parliament of man" will be ushered in. This international tribunal will be the court of appeals between the nations. Fifty years ago Bahá'u'lláh wrote to all the rulers of the world about this international tribunal of arbitral justice.

These are some of the teachings in the religion of Bahá'u'lláh—all of which would take a great deal of time to expound. I will just add that it is my hope that during these days in which this Peace Conference* is discussing negotiations for terms of peace, you will strive to the utmost that peace measures and peaceful negotiations may be carried on among them.[28]

Consider how discord and dissension have prevailed in this great human family for thousands of years. Its members have ever been engaged in war and bloodshed. Up to the present time in history the world of humanity has neither attained nor enjoyed any measure of peace, owing to incessant conditions of hostility and strife. History is a continuous and consecutive record of warfare brought about by religious, sectarian, racial, patriotic and political causes. The world of humanity has found no rest. Mankind has always been in conflict, engaged in destroying the foundations,

*Held in London during the armistice of the Balkan-Turkish War, 1912.

pillaging the properties and possessing the lands and territory of each other, especially in the earlier periods of savagery and barbarism where whole races and peoples were carried away captive by their conquerors. Who shall measure or estimate the tremendous destruction of human life resulting from this hostility and strife? What human powers and forces have been employed in the prosecution of war and applied to inhuman purposes of battle and bloodshed? In this most radiant century it has become necessary to divert these energies and utilize them in other directions, to seek the new path of fellowship and unity, to unlearn the science of war and devote supreme human forces to the blessed arts of peace. After long trial and experience we are convinced of the harmful and satanic outcomes of dissension; now we must seek after means by which the benefits of agreement and concord may be enjoyed. When such means are found, we must give them a trial. . . .

Bahá'u'lláh has proclaimed and provided the way by which hostility and dissension may be removed from the human world. He has left no ground or possibility for strife and disagreement.

First, He has proclaimed the oneness of mankind and specialized religious teachings for existing human conditions. The first form of

dissension arises from religious differences.
Bahá'u'lláh has given full teachings to the world
which are conducive to fellowship and unity in
religion. Throughout past centuries each system
of religious belief has boasted of its own
superiority and excellence, abasing and scorning
the validity of all others. Each has proclaimed
its own belief as the light and all others as
darkness. Religionists have considered the world
of humanity as two trees: one divine and merciful, the other satanic; they themselves the
branches, leaves and fruit of the divine tree and
all others who differ from them in belief the
product of the tree which is satanic. Therefore,
sedition and warfare, bloodshed and strife have
been continuous among them. The greatest
cause of human alienation has been religion
because each party has considered the belief of
the other as anathema and deprived of the
mercy of God.

The teachings specialized in Bahá'u'lláh are
addressed to humanity. He says, "Ye are all the
leaves of one tree." He does not say, "Ye are
the leaves of two trees: one divine, the other
satanic." He has declared that each individual
member of the human family is a leaf or branch
upon the Adamic tree; that all are sheltered
beneath the protecting mercy and providence of

God; that all are the children of God, fruit upon the one tree of His love. God is equally compassionate and kind to all the leaves, branches and fruit of this tree. Therefore, there is no satanic tree whatever—Satan being a product of human minds and of instinctive human tendencies toward error. God alone is Creator, and all are creatures of His might. Therefore, we must love mankind as His creatures, realizing that all are growing upon the tree of His mercy, servants of His omnipotent will and manifestations of His good pleasure. . . .

Another cause of dissension and disagreement is the fact that religion has been pronounced at variance with science. Between scientists and the followers of religion there has always been controversy and strife for the reason that the latter have proclaimed religion superior in authority to science and considered scientific announcement opposed to the teachings of religion. Bahá'u'lláh declared that religion is in complete harmony with science and reason. If religious belief and and doctrine is at variance with reason, it proceeds from the limited mind of man and not from God; therefore, it is unworthy of belief and not deserving of attention; the heart finds no rest in it, and real faith is impossible. How can man believe that which he knows to be opposed to reason? Is this possible? Can the heart accept that which reason denies? Reason is the first faculty of man, and the religion of God is in harmony with it. Bahá'u'lláh has removed this form of dissension and discord from among mankind and reconciled science with religion by revealing the pure teachings of the divine reality. This accomplishment is specialized to Him in this Day.

Still another cause of disagreement and dissension has been the formation of religious sects and denominations. Bahá'u'lláh said that God has sent religion for the purpose of establishing fellowship among humankind and not to create strife and discord, for all religion is founded upon the love of humanity. Abraham promulgated this principle, Moses summoned all to its recognition, Christ established it, and Muḥammad directed mankind to its standard. This is the reality of religion. If we abandon hearsay and investigate the reality and inner significance of the heavenly teachings, we will find the same divine foundation of love for humanity. The purport is that religion is intended to be the cause of unity, love and fellowship and not discord, enmity and estrangement. Man has forsaken the foundation of divine religion and adhered to blind imitations.

Each nation has clung to its own imitations, and because these are at variance, warfare, bloodshed and destruction of the foundation of humanity have resulted. True religion is based upon love and agreement. Bahá'u'lláh has said, "If religion and faith are the causes of enmity and sedition, it is far better to be nonreligious, and the absence of religion would be preferable; for we desire religion to be the cause of amity and fellowship. If enmity and hatred exist, irreligion is preferable." Therefore, the removal of this dissension has been specialized in Bahá'u'lláh, for religion is the divine remedy for human antagonism and discord. But when we make the remedy the cause of the disease, it would be better to do without the remedy.

Other sources of human dissension are political, racial and patriotic prejudices. These have been removed by Bahá'u'lláh. He has said, and has guarded His statement by rational proofs from the Holy Books, that the world of humanity is one race, the surface of the earth one place of residence and that these imaginary racial barriers and political boundaries are without right or foundation. Man is degraded in becoming the captive of his own illusions and suppositions. The earth is one earth, and the same atmosphere surrounds it. No difference or preference has been made by God for its human inhabitants; but man has laid the foundation of prejudice, hatred and discord with his fellowman by considering nationalities separate in importance and races different in rights and privileges.

Diversity of languages has been a fruitful cause of discord. The function of language is to convey the thought and purpose of one to another. Therefore, it matters not what language man speaks or employs. Sixty years ago Bahá'u'lláh advocated one language as the greatest means of unity and the basis of international conference. He wrote to the kings and rulers of the various nations, recommending that one language should be sanctioned and adopted by all governments. According to this each nation should acquire the universal language in addition to its native tongue. The world would then be in close communication, consultation would become general, and dissensions due to diversity of speech would be removed.

Another teaching of Bahá'u'lláh is in relation to universal peace: that all mankind must be awakened to and become conscious of the harm of war, that they should be brought to realize the benefits of peace and know that peace is from God while warfare is satanic. Man must emulate the merciful God and turn away from satanic promptings in order that universal inclination shall be toward peace, love and unity and the discord of war vanish.

Lack of equality between man and woman is, likewise, a cause of human dissension. Bahá'u'lláh has named this as an important factor of discord and separation, for so long as humankind remains unequally divided in right and importance between male and female, no unity can be established. In a perfect human body it is not possible for one organ to be complete and another defective. In the great body of human society it is impossible to establish unity and coordination if one part is considered perfect and the other imperfect. When the perfect functions of both parts are in operation, harmony will prevail. God has created man and woman equal as to faculties. He has made no distinction between them. Woman has not reached the level of man in human accomplishment because of the lack of opportunity and education. If educational opportunities were made equal and similar, the two parts, man and woman, would equalize in attainment. God has intended no difference between them that should be productive of discord. He has endowed all with human faculties, and all are manifestations of His mercy. If we say man and woman differ in creational endowment, it is contrary to divine justice and intention. Both are human. If God has created one perfect and the other defective, He is unjust. But God is just; all are perfect in His intention and creative endowment. To assume imperfection in the creature is to presuppose imperfection in the almighty Creator. The soul that excels in attainment of His attributes and graces is most acceptable before God.[29]

The Means to Eliminate War

"By what process . . . will this peace on earth be established? Will it come at once after a universal declaration of the truth?"

"No, it will come about gradually," said 'Abdu'l-Bahá. "A plant that grows too quickly lasts but a short time. You are my family" and he looked about with a smile, "my new children! If a family lives in unison, great results are obtained. Widen the circle; when a city lives in intimate accord greater results will follow, and a continent that is fully united will likewise unite all other continents. Then will be the time of the greatest results, for all the inhabitants of the earth belong to one native land."[30]

The ideals of Peace must be nurtured and spread among the inhabitants of the world; they must be instructed in the school of Peace and the evils of war. First: The financiers and bankers must desist from lending money to any government contemplating to wage an unjust war upon an innocent nation. Second: The presidents and managers of the railroads and steamship companies must refrain from transporting war ammunition, infernal engines, guns, cannons and powder from one country into another. Third: The soldiers must petition, through their representatives, the Ministers of War, the politicians, the Congressmen and the generals to put forth in a clear, intelligible language the reasons and the causes which have brought them to the brink of

65

such a national calamity. The soldiers must *demand* this as one of the prerogatives. "Demonstrate to us," they must say, "that this is a just war, and we will then enter into the battlefield otherwise we will not take one step. O ye kings and rulers, politicians and war-mongers; ye who spend your lives in most exquisite palaces of Italian architecture; ye who sleep in airy, well-ventilated apartments; ye who decorate your reception and dining halls with lovely pictures, sculptures, hangings and frescoes; ye who walk in perfect elysiums, wreathed in orange and myrtle groves, the air redolent with delicious perfumes and vocal with the sweet songs of a thousand birds, the earth like a luxuriant carpet of emerald grass, bright flowers dotting the meadows and trees clothed in verdure; ye who are dressed in costly silk and finely-woven textures; ye who lie down on soft, feathery couches; ye who partake of the most delicious and savoury dishes; ye who enjoy the utmost ease and comfort in your wondrous mansions; ye who attend rare musical concerts whenever you feel a little disconcerted and sad; ye who adorn your large halls with green festoons and cut flowers, fresh garlands and verdant wreaths, illumining them with thousands of electric lights, while the exquisite fragrance of the flowers, the soft, ravishing music, the fairy-like illumination, lends enchantment; ye who are in such environment: Come forth from your hiding-places, enter into the battlefield if you like to attack each other and tear each other to pieces if you desire to air your so-called contentions. The discord and feud are between you; why do you make us, innocent people, a party to it? If fighting and bloodshed are good things, then lead us into the fray by your presence!''

In short, every means that produces war must be checked and the causes that prevent the occurrence of war be advanced;—so that physical conflict may become an impossibility. On the other hand, every country must be properly delimited, its exact frontiers marked, its national integrity secured, its permanent independence protected, and its vital interests honored by the family of nations. These services ought to be rendered by an impartial, international Commission. In this manner all causes of friction and differences will be removed. And in case there should arise some disputes between them, they could arbitrate before the Parliament of Man, the representatives of which should be chosen from among the wisest and most judicious men of all the nations of the world.[31]

$\mathcal{B}$y a general agreement all the governments of the world must disarm simultaneously and at the same time. It will not do if one lays down the arms and the other refuses to do so. The nations of the world must concur with each other concerning this supremely important subject, thus they may abandon together the deadly weapons of human slaughter. As long as one nation increases her military and naval budget, another nation will be forced into this crazed competition through her natural and supposed interests. For example, Germany has unceasingly added to a vast sum for the maintenance of her army; this alarms the French statesmen and volatile patriots, and affects the calm and steady nerves of the Britishers across the channel. Immediately there will be rumors of war; German aggression, German ambition, the yellow journals write scaring editorials, jingoism becomes the topic of the capitals and the air will be filled with suspicions. Someone will see, for the purpose of expediency, a German dirigible flying over French fortifications or English forts, making observations, whereupon a hue and a cry will be raised from every quarter of the country, and thus there will be a corresponding increase in the estimates of the Minister of War for the defense of our homes and our hearths, our women and our sweethearts, from the attacks of strangers! The same argument is resorted to when the French nation adds one or two years to her military conscription, and the English Imperialists emphasize in public meetings the doctrine of the "double standard power." Now as long as Germany continues in her own military perfection, the French will walk in her footsteps, trying at every turn to increase their own war ammunition, to be prepared for any national crisis or sudden attack. Hence, it seems, the only solution lies in the fact of universal disarmament on the part of the nations. . . .

Now the question of disarmament must be put into practice by all the nations and not only by one or two. Consequently the advocates of Peace must strive day and night, so that the individuals of every country may become peace-loving, public opinion may gain a strong and permanent footing, and day by day the army of International Peace be increased, complete disarmament be realized and the Flag of Universal Conciliation be waving on the summit of the mountains of the earth.[32]

Another fact of equal importance in bringing about International Peace is Woman's Suffrage. That is to say, when perfect equality shall be established between men and women, peace may be realized for the simple reason that womankind in general will never favor warfare. Women evidently will not be willing to allow those whom they have so tenderly cared for to go to the battlefield. When they shall have a vote they will oppose any cause of warfare. Another factor which will bring about universal peace is the linking together of the Orient and the Occident.[33]

The most momentous question of this day is international peace and arbitration, and universal peace is impossible without universal suffrage. Children are educated by the women. The mother bears the troubles and anxieties of rearing the child, undergoes the ordeal of its birth and training. Therefore, it is most difficult for mothers to send to the battlefield those upon whom they have lavished such love and care. Consider a son reared and trained twenty years by a devoted mother. What sleepless nights and restless, anxious days she has spent! Having brought him through dangers and difficulties to the age of maturity, how agonizing then to sacrifice him upon the battlefield! Therefore, the mothers will not sanction war nor be satisfied with it. So it will come to pass that when women participate fully and equally in the affairs of the world, when they enter confidently and capably the great arena of laws and politics, war will cease; for woman will be the obstacle and hindrance to it. This is true and without doubt.[34]

I desire you for distinction. The Bahá'ís must be distinguished from others of humanity. But this distinction must not depend upon wealth—that they should become more affluent than other people. I do not desire for you financial distinction. It is not an ordinary distinction I desire; not scientific, commercial, industrial distinction. For you I desire spiritual distinction; that is, you must become eminent and distinguished in morals. In the Love of God you must become distinguished from all else. You must become distinguished for loving humanity; for unity and accord; for love and justice. In brief, you must become distinguished in all the virtues of the human world; for faithfulness and sincerity; for justice and fidelity; for firmness and steadfastness; for philanthropic deeds and service to the human world; for love toward every human being; for unity and accord with all people; for removing prejudices and promoting International Peace. Finally, you must become distinguished for heavenly illumination and acquiring the bestowals of God. I desire this distinction for you. This must be the point of distinction among you.[35]

On World Government

Note ye how easily, where unity existeth in a given family, the affairs of that family are conducted; what progress the members of that family make, how they prosper in the world. Their concerns are in order, they enjoy comfort and tranquility, they are secure, their position is assured, they come to be envied by all. Such a family but addeth to its stature and its lasting honor, as day succeedeth day. And if we widen out the sphere of unity a little to include the inhabitants of a village who seek to be loving and united, who associate with and are kind to one another, what great advances they will be seen to make, how secure and protected they will be. Then let us widen out the sphere a little more, let us take the inhabitants of a city, all of them together: if they establish the strongest bonds of unity among themselves, how far they will progress, even in a brief period and what power they will exert. And if the sphere of unity be still further widened out, that is, if the inhabitants of a whole country develop peaceable hearts, and if with all their hearts and souls they yearn to cooperate with one another and to live in unity, and if they become kind and loving to one another, that country will achieve undying joy and lasting glory. Peace will it have, and plenty, and vast wealth.

Note then: if every clan, tribe, community, every nation, country, territory on earth should come together under the single-hued pavilion of the oneness of mankind, and by the dazzling rays of the Sun of Truth should proclaim the universality of man; if they should cause all nations and all creeds to open wide their arms to one another, establish a World Council, and proceed to bind the members of society one to another by strong mutual ties, what would happen then? There is no doubt whatsoever that the divine Beloved, in all His endearing beauty, and with Him a massive host of heavenly confirmations and human blessings and bestowals, would appear in His full glory before the assemblage of the world.[36]

𝒯rue civilization will unfurl its banner in the midmost heart of the world whenever a certain number of its distinguished and high-minded sovereigns—the shining exemplars of devotion and determination—shall, for the good and happiness of all mankind, arise, with firm resolve and clear vision, to establish the Cause of Universal Peace. They must make the Cause of Peace the object of general consultation, and seek by every means

in their power to establish a Union of the
nations of the world. They must conclude a
binding treaty and establish a covenant, the provisions of which shall be sound, inviolable and
definite. They must proclaim it to all the world
and obtain for it the sanction of all the human
race. This supreme and noble undertaking—the
real source of the peace and well-being of all the
world—should be regarded as sacred by all that
dwell on earth. All the forces of humanity must
be mobilized to ensure the stability and permanence of this Most Great Covenant. In this
all-embracing Pact the limits and frontiers of
each and every nation should be clearly fixed,
the principles underlying the relations of governments towards one another definitely laid down,
and all international agreements and obligations
ascertained. In like manner, the size of the
armaments of every government should be
strictly limited, for if the preparations for war
and the military forces of any nation should be
allowed to increase, they will arouse the suspi-
cion of others. The fundamental principle
underlying this solemn Pact should be so fixed
that if any government later violate any one of
its provisions, all the governments on earth
should arise to reduce it to utter submission,
nay the human race as a whole should resolve,

with every power at its disposal, to destroy that
government. Should this greatest of all remedies
be applied to the sick body of the world, it will
assuredly recover from its ills and will remain
eternally safe and secure.[37]

. . . Although the League of
Nations has been brought into existence, yet it
is incapable of establishing universal peace. But
the Supreme Tribunal which Bahá'u'lláh has
described will fulfil this sacred task with the utmost might and power. And His plan is this:
that the national assemblies of each country and
nation—that is to say parliaments—should elect
two or three persons who are the choicest men
of that nation, and are well informed concerning international laws and the relations between
governments and aware of the essential needs of
the world of humanity in this day. The number
of these representatives should be in proportion
to the number of inhabitants of that country.
The election of these souls who are chosen by
the national assembly, that is, the parliament,

must be confirmed by the upper house, the congress and the cabinet and also by the president or monarch so these persons may be the elected ones of all the nation and the government. From among these people the members of the Supreme Tribunal will be elected, and all mankind will thus have a share therein, for every one of these delegates is fully representative of his nation. When the Supreme Tribunal gives a ruling on any international question, either unanimously or by majority rule, there will no longer be any pretext for the plaintiff or ground of objection for the defendant. In case any of the governments or nations, in the execution of the irrefutable decision of the Supreme Tribunal, be negligent or dilatory, the rest of the nations will rise up against it, because all the governments and nations of the world are the supporters of this Supreme Tribunal. Consider what a firm foundation this is! But by a limited and restricted League the purpose will not be realized as it ought and should. This is the truth about the situation, which has been stated. . . .[38]

A few, unaware of the power latent in human endeavor, consider this matter as highly impracticable, nay even beyond the scope of man's utmost efforts. Such is not the case, however. On the contrary, thanks to the unfailing grace of God, the loving-kindness of His favored ones, the unrivaled endeavors of wise and capable souls, and the thoughts and ideas of the peerless leaders of this age, nothing whatsoever can be regarded as unattainable. Endeavor, ceaseless endeavor, is required. Nothing short of an indomitable determination can possibly achieve it. Many a cause which past ages have regarded as purely visionary, yet in this day has become most easy and practicable. Why should this most great and lofty Cause—the day-star of the firmament of true civilization and the cause of the glory, the advancement, the well-being and the success of all humanity—be regarded as impossible of achievement?[39]

From the Writings of
Shoghi Effendi

$\mathcal{L}$et there be no mistake. The principle of the Oneness of Mankind—the pivot round which all the teachings of Bahá'u'lláh revolve—is no mere outburst of ignorant emotionalism or an expression of vague and pious hope. Its appeal is not to be merely identified with a reawakening of the spirit of brotherhood and good-will among men, nor does it aim solely at the fostering of harmonious cooperation among individual peoples and nations. Its implications are deeper, its claims greater than any which the Prophets of old were allowed to advance. Its message is applicable not only to the individual, but concerns itself primarily with the nature of those essential relationships that must bind all the states and nations as members of one human family. It does not constitute merely the enunciation of an ideal, but stands inseparably associated with an institution adequate to embody its truth, demonstrate its validity, and perpetuate its influence. It implies an organic change in the structure of present-day society, a change such as the world has not yet experienced. It constitutes a challenge, at once bold and universal, to outworn shibboleths of national creeds—creeds that have had their day and which must, in the ordinary course of events as shaped and controlled by Providence, give way to a new gospel, fundamentally different from, and infinitely superior to, what the world has already conceived. It calls for no less than the reconstruction and the demilitarization of the whole civilized world—a world organically unified in all the essential aspects of its life, its political machinery, its spiritual aspiration, its trade and finance, its script and language, and yet infinite in the diversity of the national characteristics of its federated units.

It represents the consummation of human evolution—an evolution that has had its earliest beginnings in the birth of family life, its subsequent development in the achievement of tribal solidarity, leading in turn to the constitution of the city-state, and expanding later into the institution of independent and sovereign nations.

The principle of the Oneness of Mankind, as proclaimed by Bahá'u'lláh, carries with it no more and no less than a solemn assertion that attainment to this final stage in this stupendous evolution is not only necessary but inevitable, that its realization is fast approaching, and that nothing short of a power that is born of God can succeed in establishing it.[40]

$\mathcal{U}$nification of the whole of mankind is the hall-mark of the stage which human society is now approaching. Unity of family, of tribe, of city-state, and nation have been successively attempted and fully established. World unity is the goal towards which a harassed humanity is striving. Nation-building has come to an end. The anarchy inherent in state sovereignty is moving towards a climax. A world, growing to maturity, must abandon this fetish, recognize the oneness and wholeness of human relationships, and establish once for all the machinery that can best incarnate this fundamental principle of its life.[41]

$\mathcal{T}$he unity of the human race, as envisaged by Bahá'u'lláh, implies the establishment of a world commonwealth in which all nations, races, creeds and classes are closely and permanently united, and in which the autonomy of its state members and the personal freedom and initiative of the individuals that compose them are definitely and completely safeguarded. This commonwealth must, as far as we can visualize it, consist of a world legislature, whose members will, as the trustees of the whole of mankind, ultimately control the entire resources of all the component nations, and will enact such laws as shall be required to regulate the life, satisfy the needs and adjust the relationships of all races and peoples. A world executive, backed by an international Force, will carry out the decisions arrived at, and apply the laws enacted by, this world legislature, and will safeguard the organic unity of the whole commonwealth. A world tribunal will adjudicate and deliver its compulsory and final verdict in all and any disputes that may arise between the various elements constituting this universal system. A mechanism of world inter-communication will be devised, embracing the whole planet, freed from national hindrances and restrictions, and functioning with marvelous swiftness and perfect regularity. A world metropolis will act as the nerve center of a world civilization, the focus towards which the unifying forces of life will converge and from which its energizing influences will radiate. A world language will either be invented or chosen from among the existing languages and will be taught

ternal order within their respective dominions. Such a state will have to include within its orbit an International Executive adequate to enforce supreme and unchallengeable authority on every recalcitrant member of the commonwealth; a World Parliament whose members shall be elected by the people in their respective countries and whose election shall be confirmed by their respective governments; and a Supreme Tribunal whose judgment will have a binding effect even in such cases where the parties concerned did not voluntarily agree to submit their case to its consideration. A world community in which all economic barriers will have been permanently demolished and the interdependence of Capital and Labor definitely recognized; in which the clamor of religious fanaticism and strife will have been forever stilled; in which the flame of racial animosity will have been finally extinguished; in which a single code of international law—the product of the considered judgment of the world's federated representatives—shall have as its sanction the instant and coercive intervention of the combined forces of the federated units; and finally a world community in which the fury of a capricious and militant nationalism will have been transmuted into an abiding consciousness of world citizenship—such indeed, appears, in its broadest outline, the Order anticipated by Bahá'u'lláh, an Order that shall come to be regarded as the fairest fruit of a slowly maturing age.

"*The Tabernacle of Unity*," Bahá'u'lláh proclaims in His message to all mankind, "*has been raised; regard ye not one another as strangers. . . . Of one tree are all ye the fruit and of one bough the leaves. . . . The world is but one country and mankind its citizens. . . . Let not a man glory in that he loves his country; let him rather glory in this, that he loves his kind.*"[43]

*L*et there be no misgivings as to the animating purpose of the world-wide Law of Bahá'u'lláh. Far from aiming at the subversion of the existing foundations of society, it seeks to broaden its basis, to remold its institutions in a manner consonant with the needs of an ever-changing world. It can conflict with no legitimate allegiances, nor can it undermine essential loyalties. Its purpose is neither to stifle the flame of a sane and intelligent patriotism in men's hearts, nor to abolish the system of national autonomy so essential if the evils of excessive centralization are to be avoided. It does not ignore, nor does it attempt to suppress, the diversity of ethnical origins, of climate, of history, of language and tradition, of thought and habit, that differentiate the peoples and nations of the world. It calls for a wider loyalty, for a larger aspiration than any that has animated the human race. It insists upon the subordination of national impulses and interests to the imperative claims of a unified world. It repudiates excessive centralization on one hand, and disclaims all attempts at uniformity on the other. Its watchword is unity in diversity. . . .

The call of Bahá'u'lláh is primarily directed against all forms of provincialism, all insularities and prejudices. If long-cherished ideals and time-honored institutions, if certain social assumptions and religious formulae have ceased to promote the welfare of the generality of mankind, if they no longer minister to the needs of a continually evolving humanity, let them be swept away and relegated to the limbo of obsolescent and forgotten doctrines. Why should these, in a world subject to the immutable law of change and decay, be exempt from the deterioration that must needs overtake every human institution? For legal standards, political and economic theories are solely designed to safeguard the interests of humanity as a whole, and not humanity to be crucified for the preservation of the integrity of any particular law or doctrine.[44]

REFERENCES

$\mathcal{P}$eace has been a central teaching of the Bahá'í Faith since its inception in 1863. Bahá'u'lláh Himself (1817-1892), the Founder of the religion, in hundreds of passages spanning the whole period of His Revelation has addressed this issue. Universal peace was the major theme of 'Abdu'l-Bahá (Bahá'u'lláh's successor and the head of the Bahá'í Faith, 1892-1921) during his journeys to Europe and America in the early 1910s. Many of his public addresses were devoted entirely to this subject; unnumbered Tablets to individuals, to journals, to peace organizations, expound on the idea of world peace. Likewise, world peace and world unity are important topics found in the major writings of Shoghi Effendi, the Guardian of the Bahá'í Faith from 1921 to 1957.

This compilation then is only a small selection from an ocean of Bahá'í scripture and interpretation. It should be regarded as only a beginning point for further study of the subject, or as a bare introduction.

While world peace is a central teaching of the Bahá'í Faith, it would certainly be a mistake to regard the Faith as a peace movement per se. It is explicitly stated in the Bahá'í teachings that world peace (that is, the Lesser Peace, or the political peace among nations) will come about through the efforts of various groups and nations, and independent of any Bahá'í plan or effort. It is only after the previous establishment of world peace that Bahá'ís will be able to bring about the Most Great Peace—that is, to establish the moral and spiritual foundations, and the divine institutions, that will bring depth and permanence to the political cease-fire.

It is for the Most Great Peace that Bahá'ís and Bahá'í institutions are working. Their aim is nothing less than the spiritual transformation of the future world civilization. As they go about this work of changing the values and the spiritual vision of mankind, it is nonetheless their duty also to lend their aid to those agencies outside the Bahá'í religion that are working for the Lesser Peace. As Shoghi Effendi, in a letter written on his behalf, put it:

> The Cause will not attain its aim and order in the great reign of peace unless its principles are put into practice. We have to assist the different movements which have progressive ideas and are striving for an aim similar to ours.
>
> We have to help every such society even if it is merely to abolish the prejudice and ill feeling which prevails . . . Provided always that we do not entangle the Cause in political issues and party affiliations. (*Bahá'í News,* no. 10, February 1926, p. 7)

The few selections from the Bahá'í writings that we have quoted above are from the following sources:

From the Writings of Bahá'u'lláh

1. From Lawḥ-i Maqṣúd. *Gleanings from the Writings of Bahá'u'lláh, pp. 218-19.* Cf. *The Revelation of Bahá'u'lláh,* p. 270.
2. From Lawḥ-i Maqṣúd. *Gleanings from the Writings of Bahá'u'lláh,* p. 249.
3. From a Tablet to Queen Victoria. *Gleanings from the Writings of Bahá'u'lláh,* pp. 253-54.
4. From Lawḥ-i Maqṣúd. *Gleanings from the Writings of Bahá'u'lláh,* p. 250.
5. From a Tablet to Mánikchí Sáhib. *Gleanings from the Writings of Bahá'u'lláh,* p. 213. Cf. *The Revelation of Bahá'u'lláh,* vol. 3, p. 213.

From the Words of 'Abdu'l-Bahá

6. From a Tablet to the Executive Committee of the Central Organization for a Durable Peace, The Hague, December 17, 1919. *Selections from the Writings of 'Abdu'l-Bahá,* pp. 296-97.
7. From a Tablet addressed to the readers of *The Christian Commonwealth,* January 1, 1913. *Selections from the Writings of 'Abdu'l-Bahá,* p. 276.
8. From a Tablet addressed to the maid-servant of God, Miss Beatrice Irwin, London. Translated by Mirza Ahmad Sohrab, October 4, 1914. *Star of the West,* vol. 5, no. 16 (December 31, 1914) pp. 244-45.
9. From the Diary of Mirza Ahmad Sohrab. Questions asked and answers given by 'Abdu'l-Bahá, May 11-14, 1914. *Star of the West,* vol. 5, no. 8 (August 1, 1914) p. 115.
10. From a talk given in Paris, October 21, 1912. *Paris Talks,* pp. 28-29.
11. From an interview of Hudson Maxim with 'Abdu'l-Bahá at the Hotel Ansonia, New York City, April 15, 1912. Notes by

Howard MacNutt. *Star of the West,* vol. 3, no. 7 (July 13, 1912) pp. 5 and 10.

12. From a talk given in Haifa, August 3, 1914. From the Diary of Mirza Ahmad Sohrab. *Star of the West,* vol. 5, no. 11 (September 27, 1914) pp. 165-66.

13. From a talk given at Stanford University, Palo Alto, California, October 8, 1912. Notes by Bijou Straun. *The Promulgation of Universal Peace,* pp. 354-55.

14. From an address given at Pembroke Chapel, Liverpool, England, December 15, 1912. Notes by Isabel Fraser. *Star of the West,* vol. 3, no. 17 (January 19, 1913) pp. 4-5.

15. From a talk given at Stanford University, Palo Alto, California, October 8, 1912. Notes by Bijou Straun. *The Promulgation of Universal Peace,* p. 354.

16. From a talk given to the Theosophical Society, Paris, 1912. *Paris Talks,* p. 130.

17. From a Tablet addressed to the maid-servant of God, Miss Beatrice Irwin, London. Translated by Mirza Ahmad Sohrab, October 14, 1914. *Star of the West,* vol. 5, no. 16 (December 31, 1914) p. 244.

18. From *The Secret of Divine Civilization,* p. 61.

19. From a Tablet to the Editor of *The Christian Commonwealth,* London. Translated by Mirza Ahmad Sohrab, July 19, 1913. *Star of the West,* vol. 5, no. 8 (August 1, 1914) p. 120.

20. Extract from a Tablet to an American believer, September 12, 1911. *9 Compilation of the Holy Utterances of Baha'o'llah and Abdul Baha Concerning the Most Great Peace, War and Duty of the Bahais toward their Government,* p. 74.

21. From a Tablet to the Editor of *The Christian Commonwealth,* London, 1913. *Star of the West,* vol. 5, no. 8 (August 1, 1914) p. 121.

22. From a talk given at a meeting of the international Peace Forum, Grace Methodist Episcopal Church, New York City, May 12, 1912. Notes by Esther Foster. *The Promulgation of Universal Peace,* p. 121.

23. From a talk given in Paris, November 19, 1912. *Paris Talks,* pp. 100-101.

24. From an interview of W. H. Short, secretary of the New York Peace Society, with 'Abdu'l-Bahá, Hotel Ansonia, New

York City, April 15, 1912. Notes by Howard MacNutt. *Star of the West,* vol. 3, no. 7 (July 13, 1912) p. 4.

25. From *The Secret of Divine Civilization,* pp. 61-63.

26. From a talk to an American newspaper correspondent on board the Cedric as 'Abdu'l-Bahá approached America. From the Diary of Mirza Ahmad Sohrab, July 20, 1913. *9 Compilation of the Holy Utterances of Baha'o'llah and Abdul Baha Concerning the Most Great Peace, War and Duty of the Bahais toward their Government,* p. 130.

27. From a talk given by 'Abdu'l-Bahá at Clifton, England, January 16, 1913. Notes by Isabel Fraser. *Star of the West,* vol. 4, no.1 (March 21, 1913) pp. 5-6.

28. From an address given at the Westminster Palace Hotel, London, December 20, 1912. Notes by Isabel Fraser. *Star of the West,* vol. 3, no. 17 (January 19, 1913) pp. 6-8.

29. From a talk given at All Souls Unitarian Church, July 14, 1912. Notes by John G. Grundy and Howard MacNutt. *The Promulgation of Universal Peace,* pp. 229-33.

30. From "Days in London." *Abdul Baha in London: Addresses, & Notes of Conversations,* pp. 109-110.

31. From the Diary of Mirza Ahmad Sohrab. Questions asked of and answers given by 'Abdu'l-Bahá, May 11-14, 1914. *Star of the West,* vol. 5, no. 8 (August 1, 1914) pp. 116-17.

32. Ibid., p. 116.

33. From an address to the Protestant Episcopal Church of the Ascension, New York City, June 2, 1912. *Star of the West,* Vol. 3, no. 10 (September 8, 1912) p. 27.

34. From a talk given at a Woman's Suffrage Meeting, Metropolitan Temple, New York City, May 20, 1912. Notes by Esther Foster. *The Promulgation of Universal Peace,* pp. 134-35.

35. From a talk given in New York City, June 15, 1912. Notes by Howard MacNutt. *Star of the West,* vol. 3, no. 10 (September 8, 1912) p. 17.

36. From *Selections from the Writings of 'Abdu'l-Bahá,* p. 279-80.

37. From *The Secret of Divine Civilization,* pp. 64-65.

38. From a Tablet to the Executive Committee of the Central Organization for a Durable Peace, The Hague, December 17, 1919. *Selections from the Writings of 'Abdu'l-Bahá,* pp. 306-307.

39. From *The Secret of Divine Civilization,* p. 66.

REFERENCES

From the Writings of Shoghi Effendi

40. From "The Goal of a New World Order," November 28, 1931. *The World Order of Bahá'u'lláh,* pp. 42-43.
41. From "The Unfoldment of World Civilization," March 11, 1936. *The World Order of Bahá'u'lláh,* p. 202.
42. Ibid., pp. 203-204.
43. From "The Goal of a New World Order." *The World Order of Bahá'u'lláh,* pp. 40-41.
44. Ibid., pp. 41-42.

ANTHONY A. LEE, COMPILER